POCKET
BOOK
-> *of* <-
PRAYERS

POCKET BOOK *of* PRAYERS

*Compiled and Edited
by Mark Gilroy*

FALL RIVER PRESS

New York

FALL RIVER PRESS

New York

An Imprint of Sterling Publishing
1166 Avenue of the Americas
New York, NY 10036

FALL RIVER PRESS and the distinctive Fall River Press logo are
registered trademarks of Barnes & Noble, Inc.

This compilation and its Introduction © 2015 by Fall River Press.

Endpapers © Aridi Graphics, Inc.

ISBN 978-1-4351-5819-1

Manufactured in China

2 4 6 8 10 9 7 5 3 1

www.sterlingpublishing.com

CONTENTS

INTRODUCTION

A Pocket Book of Prayers is a wonderful resource for those who want to experience the joy of conversation with God Almighty . . .

> *There is not in the world a kind of life more sweet and delightful than that of a continual conversation with God.*
>
> BROTHER LAWRENCE

It is for those who want to go deeper in their prayer life . . .

> *Grant that I may not pray alone with the mouth; help me that I may pray from the depths of my heart.*
>
> MARTIN LUTHER

It is for those that suspect that they can change the world—or at least *their* world through prayer . . .

> *God shapes the world by prayer. The more prayer there is in the world the better the world will be, the mightier the forces against evil.*
>
> E.M. BOUNDS

It is for those who have never quite been able to deliver a consistent prayer life . . .

Don't pray when you feel like it. Have an appointment with the Lord and keep it. A man is powerful on his knees.

CORRIE TEN BOOM

It is for those who feel they are missing out on divine blessings in their life . . .

Prayer is the root, the fountain, the mother of a thousand blessings.

SAINT JOHN CHRYSOSTOM

It is for those who feel lost and confused and who are looking for answers . . .

When you are in the dark, listen, and God will give you a very precious message.

OSWALD CHAMBERS

It is for those who struggle to put into words what is in their heart . . .

Groanings that cannot be uttered are often prayers that cannot be refused.

CHARLES H. SPURGEON

It is for those that want to grow in compassion and love for the world . . .

May God break my heart so completely that the whole world falls in.

MOTHER TERESA OF CALCUTTA

It is for those who are in desperate circumstances . . .

I have been driven many times upon my knees by the overwhelming conviction that I had no where else to go. My own wisdom and that of all about me seemed insufficient for that day.

ABRAHAM LINCOLN

It is for those who want to become stronger . . .

Do not pray for easier lives. Pray to be stronger men.

PHILLIPS BROOKS

It is for those who want to be honest before God . . .

It is of great importance, when we begin to practise prayer, not to let ourselves be frightened by our own thoughts.

SAINT TERESA OF AVILA

It is for those who want to experience the miraculous . . .

Learn to worship God as the God who does wonders, who wishes to prove in you that He can do something supernatural and divine.

ANDREW MURRAY

It is for those who wonder if God is real . . .

In worship, God imparts himself to us.

C.S. LEWIS

Quite simply, *A Pocket Book of Prayers* is for you. As you read the words from those who have prayed down through the ages, make them your own as you accept the invitation to converse with the Creator of the Universe.

—MARK GILROY

PRAYERS
of
PRAISE
and WORSHIP

Come, let us sing with joy to the Lord.
Let us sing loud with joy to the rock
Who saves us.

PSALM 95:1, NLT

The Lord's Prayer

Our Father in heaven,
Hallowed be Your name.
Your kingdom come.
Your will be done
On earth as it is in heaven.
Give us this day our daily bread.
And forgive us our debts,
As we forgive our debtors.
And do not lead us into temptation,
But deliver us from the evil one.
For Yours is the kingdom and the power and the glory forever.
Amen.

Matthew 6:19–21, NKJV

Hymn to Joy

Joyful, joyful, we adore Thee, God of glory, Lord of love;
Hearts unfold like flow'rs before Thee, opening to the
    sun above.
Melt the clouds of sin and sadness; drive the dark of
    doubt away.
Giver of immortal gladness, fill us with the light of day!
All Thy works with joy surround Thee, earth and heav'n
    reflect Thy rays;
Stars and angels sing around Thee, center of unbroken praise.
Field and forest, vale and mountain, flow'ry meadow,
    flashing sea;
Chanting bird and flowing fountain, call us to rejoice in Thee.
Thou art giving and forgiving, ever blessing, ever blest,

Well-spring of the joy of living, ocean-depth of happy rest!

Thou the Father, Christ our Brother, all who live in love
are Thine:

Teach us how to love each other, lift us to the Joy Divine.

Mortals join the mighty chorus, which the morning stars
began;

Father-love is reigning o'er us, brother-love binds man
to man.

Ever singing, march we onward, victors in the midst
of strife;

Joyful music lifts us sunward, in the triumph song of life.

HENRY VAN DYKE (1852–1933)
American author and minister
(Usually sung to Beethoven's *Ode to Joy*)

Shout with Joy

Shout with joy to the Lord, all the earth!

Worship the Lord with gladness.

Come before him, singing with joy.

Acknowledge that the Lord is God!

He made us, and we are his.

We are his people, the sheep of his pasture.

Enter his gates with thanksgiving; go into his courts with
praise.

Give thanks to him and praise his name.

For the Lord is good.

His unfailing love continues forever, and his faithfulness
continues to each generation.

Psalm 100, NLT

Gloria Patri

Glory be to the Father, and to the Son: and to the Holy Ghost;
As it was in the beginning, is now, and ever shall be: world
without end.
Amen.

Traditional doxology

Praise God

Praise God, from whom all blessings flow;
Praise him, all creatures here below;
Praise him above, ye heavenly host;
Praise Father, Son, and Holy Ghost. Amen.

Christian traditional

The Radiance of Your Father's Splendor

The radiance of the Father's splendor, the Father's visible
image, Jesus Christ our God, peerless among counselors,
Prince of Peace, Father of the world to come, the model
after which Adam was formed, for our sakes became like a
slave: in the womb of Mary the virgin, without assistance
from any man, he took flesh.

Enable us, Lord, to reach the end of this glorious feast
in peace, forsaking all idle words, acting virtuously,
shunning our passions, and raising ourselves above the
things of this world.

Bless your church, which you brought into being long
ago and attached to yourself through your own life-giving
blood. Help all pastors, heads of churches, and teachers.

Bless your servants, whose trust is all in you; bless all Christian souls, the sick, those tormented by evil spirits, and those who have asked us to pray for them.

Show yourself as merciful as you are rich in grace; save and preserve us; enable us to obtain those good things to come which will never know an end.

May we celebrate your glorious birth, and the Father who sent you to redeem us, and your Spirit, the Giver of life, now and forever, age after age. Amen.

A Syriac liturgy, fourth century

You Know Me

You have searched me, Lord, and you know me. You know when I sit and when I rise; you perceive my thoughts from afar. You discern my going out and my lying down; you are familiar with all my ways.

Before a word is on my tongue you, Lord, know it completely. You hem me in behind and before, and you lay your hand upon me. Such knowledge is too wonderful for me, too lofty for me to attain.

Where can I go from your Spirit? Where can I flee from your presence? If I go up to the heavens, you are there; if I make my bed in the depths, you are there. If I rise on the wings of the dawn, if I settle on the far side of the sea, even there your hand will guide me, your right hand will hold me fast.

If I say, "Surely the darkness will hide me and the light become night around me," even the darkness will not be dark to you; the night will shine like the day, for darkness is as light to you.

For you created my inmost being; you knit me together in my mother's womb. I praise you because I am fearfully and wonderfully made; your works are wonderful, I know that full well. My frame was not hidden from you when I was made in the secret place, when I was woven together in the depths of the earth. Your eyes saw my unformed body; all the days ordained for me were written in your book before one of them came to be.

How precious to me are your thoughts, God! How vast is the sum of them! Were I to count them, they would outnumber the grains of sand—when I awake, I am still with you.

Psalm 139:1–8, NIV

And Can It Be?

And can it be that I should gain
An interest in the Savior's blood?
Died He for me, who caused His pain
For me, who Him to death pursued?
Amazing love! How can it be,
That Thou, my God, shouldst die for me?

He left His Father's throne above
So free, so infinite His grace;
Emptied Himself of all but love,
And bled for Adam's helpless race;
'Tis mercy all, immense and free,
For, O my God, it found out me!

Long my imprisoned spirit lay,
Fast bound in sin and nature's night:
Thine eye diffused a quickening ray;
I woke, the dungeon flamed with light;
My chains fell off, my heart was free,
I rose, went forth, and followed Thee.

No condemnation now I dread,
Jesus, with all in Him, is mine;
Alive in Him, my living Head,
And clothed in righteousness divine,
Bold I approach th'eternal throne,
And claim the crown, through Christ my own.

CHARLES WESLEY (1707–1788)
Anglican minister and hymnist

God of Heaven and Earth

Our God, God of all men
God of heaven and earth, seas and rivers,
God of sun and moon, of all the stars,
God of high mountain and lowly valley,
God over heaven, and in heaven, and under heaven.
He has a dwelling in heaven and earth and sea
And in all things that are in them.

He inspires all things, he quickens all things.
He is over all things, he supports all things.
He makes the light of the sun to shine,

He surrounds the moon and the stars,
He has made wells in the arid earth,
Placed dry islands in the sea.

He has a Son co-eternal with himself . . .
And the Holy Spirit breathes in them;
Not separate are the Father and the Son and the Holy Spirit.

SAINT PATRICK (387–late fifth century)
Patron saint of Ireland

Glorious and Wonderful

We bless Thee, O most high God and Lord of mercy, Who art ever doing numberless great and inscrutable things with us, glorious and wonderful; Who grantest to us sleep for rest from our infirmities, and repose from the burdens of our much toiling flesh.

We thank Thee that Thou hast not destroyed us with our sins, but hast loved us as ever, and though we are sunk in despair, Thou hast raised us up to glorify Thy power.

Therefore we implore Thy incomparable goodness, enlighten the eyes of our understanding and raise up our mind from the heavy sleep of indolence; open our mouth and fill it with Thy praise, that we may be able undistracted to sing and confess Thee, Who art God glorified in all and by all, the eternal Father, with Thy only-begotten Son, and Thy all-holy and good and life-giving Spirit, now and ever, and to the ages of ages.

Amen.

SAINT BASIL THE GREAT (330–379)
Greek bishop of Caesarea

Thou Art Supremely Glorified

O All-Ruler, Word of the Father, Jesus Christ, Thou Who art perfect, never in Thy great mercy leave me, but ever abide in me, Thy servant.

O Jesus, Good Shepherd of Thy sheep, deliver me not to the revolt of the serpent and leave me not to the will of Satan, for the seed of corruption is in me.

Lord, adorable God, Holy King, Jesus Christ, guard me asleep by the unwaning light, Thy Holy Spirit, by Whom Thou didst sanctify Thy disciples.

O Lord, grant me, Thy unworthy servant, Thy salvation on my bed.

Enlighten my mind with the light of understanding of Thy Holy Gospel. Enlighten my soul with the love of Thy Cross. Enlighten my heart with the purity of Thy Word. Enlighten my body with Thy passionless Passion.

Keep my thoughts in Thy humility. And rouse me in good time to glorify Thee, for Thou art supremely glorified, with Thy eternal Father, and Thy most Holy Spirit forever.

Amen.

SAINT IGNATIUS (50–117)
Bishop of Antioch

Canticle of the Sun

Most high, all powerful, all good Lord! All praise is yours, all glory, all honor, and all blessing. To you, alone, Most High, do they belong. No mortal lips are worthy to pronounce your name.

Be praised, my Lord, through all your creatures, especially through my lord Brother Sun, who brings the day; and you give light through him. And he is beautiful and radiant in all his splendor! Of you, Most High, he bears the likeness.

Be praised, my Lord, through Sister Moon and the stars; in the heavens you have made them, precious and beautiful.

Be praised, my Lord, through Brothers Wind and Air, and clouds and storms, and all the weather, through which you give your creatures sustenance.

Be praised, My Lord, through Sister Water; she is very useful, and humble, and precious, and pure.

Be praised, my Lord, through Brother Fire, through whom you brighten the night. He is beautiful and cheerful, and powerful and strong.

Be praised, my Lord, through our sister Mother Earth, who feeds us and rules us, and produces various fruits with colored flowers and herbs.

Be praised, my Lord, through those who forgive for love of you; through those who endure sickness and trial. Happy are those who endure in peace, for by you, Most High, they will be crowned.

Be praised, my Lord, through our Sister Bodily Death, from whose embrace no living person can escape. Woe to those who die in mortal sin! Happy those she finds doing your most holy will. The second death can do no harm to them.

Praise and bless my Lord, and give thanks, and serve him with great humility.

SAINT FRANCIS OF ASSISI (d. 1226)
Patron saint of animals and nature

Your Power and Glory

O God, you are my God; I earnestly search for you.

My soul thirsts for you; my whole body longs for you in this parched and weary land where there is no water.

I have seen you in your sanctuary and gazed upon your power and glory.

Your unfailing love is better than life itself; how I praise you!

I will praise you as long as I live, lifting up my hands to you in prayer.

You satisfy me more than the richest feast. I will praise you with songs of joy.

I lie awake thinking of you, meditating on you through the night.

Because you are my helper, I sing for joy in the shadow of your wings.

I cling to you; your strong right hand holds me securely.

Psalm 63:1–8, NLT

Amazing Grace

Amazing Grace, how sweet the sound,
That saved a wretch like me.
I once was lost but now am found,
Was blind, but now I see.

'Twas Grace that taught my heart to fear.
And Grace, my fears relieved.
How precious did that Grace appear
The hour I first believed.

Through many dangers, toils and snares
I have already come;
'Tis Grace that brought me safe thus far
And Grace will lead me home.

The Lord has promised good to me.
His word my hope secures.
He will my shield and portion be,
As long as life endures.

Yea, when this flesh and heart shall fail,
And mortal life shall cease,
I shall possess within the veil,
A life of joy and peace.

JOHN NEWTON (1725–1807)
British "slaver" turned abolitionist

PRAYERS
→ *for* ←
FORGIVENESS
and RENEWAL

If we claim that we're free of sin, we're only fooling ourselves. A claim like that is errant nonsense. On the other hand, if we admit our sins—make a clean breast of them—he won't let us down; he'll be true to himself. He'll forgive our sins and purge us of all wrongdoing. If we claim that we've never sinned, we out-and-out contradict God— make a liar out of him. A claim like that only shows off our ignorance of God.

1 JOHN 1:8–10
The Message

A Heart to Love

O Lord, who hast mercy upon all, take away from me my sins, and mercifully kindle in me the fire of thy Holy Spirit.

Take away from me the heart of stone, and give me a heart of flesh, a heart to love and adore thee, a heart to delight in thee, to follow and to enjoy thee, for Christ's sake.

SAINT AMBROSE OF MILAN
Fourth century

Pardon My Unworthiness

O Lord, Heavenly King, Comforter, Spirit of Truth, have compassion and mercy on Thy sinful servant and pardon my unworthiness, and forgive me all the sins that I humanly committed today, and not only humanly but even worse than a beast—my voluntary sins, known and unknown, from my youth and from evil suggestions, and from my brazenness, and from boredom.

If I have sworn by Thy Name or blasphemed it in thought, blamed or reproached anyone, or in my anger have detracted or slandered anyone, or grieved anyone, or if I have got angry about anything, or have told a lie, if I have slept unnecessarily, or if a beggar has come to me and I despised or neglected him, or if I have troubled my brother or quarreled with him, or if I have condemned anyone, or have boasted, or have been proud, or lost my temper with anyone, or if when standing in prayer my mind has been distracted by the glamour of this world, or if I have had depraved thoughts or have overeaten, or have drunk excessively, or have laughed frivolously, or have thought evil, or have seen the attraction of someone and been wounded by it in my heart, or said indecent things, or made fun of my brother's sin when my own faults are countless, or been neglectful of prayer, or have done some other wrong that I cannot remember—for I have done all this and much more—have mercy, my Lord and Creator, on me Thy wretched and unworthy servant, and absolve and forgive and deliver me in Thy goodness and love for men, so that, lustful, sinful and wretched as I am, I may lie down and sleep and rest in peace.

And I shall worship, praise and glorify Thy most honorable Name, with the Father and His only-begotten Son, now and ever, and for all ages. Amen.

Saint Ephrem (306–373)
Syrian bishop and theologian

King David's Prayer

Have mercy on me, O God, according to your unfailing love; according to your great compassion blot out my transgressions.

Wash away all my iniquity and cleanse me from my sin.

For I know my transgressions, and my sin is always before me.

Against you, you only, have I sinned and done what is evil in your sight; so you are right in your verdict and justified when you judge.

Surely I was sinful at birth, sinful from the time my mother conceived me.

Yet you desired faithfulness even in the womb; you taught me wisdom in that secret place.

Cleanse me with hyssop, and I will be clean; wash me, and I will be whiter than snow.

Let me hear joy and gladness; let the bones you have crushed rejoice.

Hide your face from my sins and blot out all my iniquity.

Create in me a pure heart, O God, and renew a steadfast spirit within me.

Do not cast me from your presence or take your Holy Spirit from me.

Restore to me the joy of your salvation and grant me a willing spirit, to sustain me.

Psalm 51:1–12, NIV

Revive Thy Work

Oh Lord our God we thank thee more than ever that thou has been pleased to give us thy Holy Word. We realize what frail, fallible creatures we are, and how prone we are to go off on tangents and to trust to our own understanding only. We thank thee that thou has given us thy Spirit and thou has given us thy Word.

Oh God we cry out to thee, as a company of thy people, to have mercy upon us. God of our fathers, let it be known that thou art still God in Israel. Let it be known in this arrogant 20th Century, that thou art the same God who has acted and operated throughout the running centuries.

Honor thine own Word, oh Lord. Honor thine own dear Son. Exalt his precious name, and bring many to knowledge of him as their only Savior and their Lord.

Lord have pity upon us. In the midst of wrath remember mercy. Revive thy work, oh Lord, thy mighty arm made bare. Speak with a voice that wakes the dead, and make the people hear.

Martin Lloyd Jones (1899–1981)
British evangelical minister

Have Mercy Upon Us

O God the Father, Creator of heaven and earth,
Have mercy upon us.
O God the Son, Redeemer of the world,
Have mercy upon us.
O God the Holy Spirit, Sanctifier of the faithful,
Have mercy upon us.
O holy, blessed, and glorious Trinity, one God,
Have mercy upon us.

Remember not, Lord Christ, our offenses, nor the offenses of our forefathers; neither reward us according to our sins.

Spare us, good Lord, spare thy people, whom thou hast redeemed with thy most precious blood, and by thy mercy preserve us, forever.

Spare us, good Lord, from all evil and wickedness; from sin; from the crafts and assaults of the devil; and from everlasting damnation.

Good Lord, deliver us.

From the Great Liturgy of
The Book of Common Prayer

A Prayer for the Church

Most gracious Father, we pray to you for your holy Catholic Church.

Fill it with all truth; in all truth with all peace.

Where it is corrupt, purge it.

Where it is in error, direct it.

Where anything is amiss, reform it.

Where it is right, strengthen and defend it.

Where it is in want, provide for it.

Where it is divided, heal it and reunite it in your love;

for the sake of your Son, our Savior Jesus Christ.

WILLIAM LAUD (1573–1645)
English theologian and archbishop of Canterbury

Thy Heavenly Joys

Lord, deprive me not of Thy heavenly joys.

Lord, deliver me from eternal torments.

Lord, if I have sinned in mind or thought, in word or deed, forgive me.

Lord, deliver me from all ignorance, forgetfulness, cowardice and stony insensibility.

Lord, deliver me from every temptation.

Lord, enlighten my heart which evil desires have darkened.

Lord, I being human have sinned, but Thou being the generous God, have mercy on me, knowing the sickness of my soul.

Lord, send Thy grace to my help, that I may glorify Thy holy Name. Lord Jesus Christ, write me Thy servant in the Book of Life, and grant me a good end.

O Lord my God, even though I have done nothing good in Thy sight, yet grant me by Thy grace to make a good start.

Lord, sprinkle into my heart the dew of Thy grace.

Lord of heaven and earth remember me, Thy sinful servant, shameful and unclean, in Thy Kingdom.

O Lord, accept me in penitence.

O Lord, leave me not.

O Lord, lead me not into temptation.

O Lord, grant me good thoughts.

O Lord, grant me tears and remembrance of death and compunction.

O Lord, grant me the thought of confessing my sins.

O Lord, grant me humility, chastity and obedience.

O Lord, grant me patience, courage and meekness.

O Lord, plant in me the root of all blessings, the fear of Thee in my heart.

O Lord, grant me to love Thee with all my mind and soul, and always to do Thy will.

O Lord, protect me from certain people, and demons, and passions, and from every other harmful thing.

O Lord, Thou knowest that Thou actest as Thou wilt; may Thy will be also in me, a sinner, for blessed art Thou forever.

Amen.

Saint John Chrysostom (347–407)
Bishop of Constantinople

Cleanse Me

O Eternal God and King of all creation, Who hast granted me to arrive at this hour, forgive me the sins that I have committed today in thought, word and deed. Cleanse, O Lord, my humble soul from all defilement of flesh and spirit.

And grant me, O Lord, to pass the sleep of this night in peace, that when I rise from my bed I may please Thy most holy Name all the days of my life and conquer my flesh and the fleshless foes that war with me.

And deliver me, O Lord, from vain and frivolous thoughts, and from evil desires which defile me.

For Thine is the kingdom, the power and the glory of the Father, Son and Holy Spirit, now and ever, and to the ages of ages.

Amen.

SAINT MACARIUS THE GREAT (300–391)
Egyptian Coptic hermit and monk

I Hunger and Thirst for More

Late have I loved you, O Beauty so ancient and so new, late have I loved you!

You were within me, but I was outside, and it was there that I searched for you.

In my unloveliness I plunged into the lovely things which you created. You were with me, but I was not with you. Created things kept me from you; yet if they had not been in you they would not have been at all.

You called, you shouted, and you broke through my deafness. You flashed, you shone, and you dispelled my blindness.

You breathed your fragrance on me; I drew in breath and now I pant for you. I have tasted you, now I hunger and thirst for more. You touched me, and I burned for your peace.

Lead us, O God, from the sight of the lovely things of the world to the thought of thee their Creator; and grant that delighting in the beautiful things of thy creation, we may delight in thee, the first author of beauty and the Sovereign Lord of all thy works, blessed for evermore.

SAINT AUGUSTINE (354–430)
Christian theologian and philosopher

The Act of Contrition

O my God,

I am heartily sorry for having offended Thee, and I detest all my sins, because I dread the loss of heaven, and the pains of hell.

But most of all because they offend Thee, my God, Who are all good and deserving of all my love.

I firmly resolve, with the help of Thy grace to confess my sins, to do penance and to amend my life.

Amen.

JAMES GIBBONS (1834–1921)
Archbishop of Baltimore

All Our Sins and Shortcomings

And now at this hour will You hear the voice of our supplication. First, we ask at Your hands, great Father, complete forgiveness for all our sins and shortcomings. We hope we can say with truthfulness that we do from our heart forgive all those who have in any way trespassed against us. There lies not in our heart, we hope, a thought of enmity towards any man. However we have been slandered or wronged, we would, with our inmost heart, forgive and forget it all.

We come to You and pray that, for Jesus's sake, and through the virtue of the blood once shed for many for the remission of sins, You would give us perfect pardon of every sin of the past. Blot out, O God, all our sins like a cloud, and let them never be seen again. Grant us also the peace-speaking word of promise supplied by the Holy Spirit, that being justified by faith we may have peace with God through Jesus Christ our Lord. Let us be forgiven and know it, and may there remain no lingering question in our heart about our reconciliation with God, but by a firm, full assurance based on faith in the finished work of Christ may we stand as forgiven men and women against whom transgression shall never be mentioned forever again.

CHARLES H. SPURGEON (1834–1892)
British Baptist preacher and author

Renew Me

Lord Jesus Christ; Let me seek you by desiring you, and let me desire you by seeking you.

Let me find you by loving you, and love you in finding you.

I confess, Lord, with thanksgiving, that you have made me in your image. So that I can remember you, think of you, and love you. But that image is so worn and blotted out by faults, and darkened by the smoke of sin, that it cannot do that for which it was made, unless you renew and refashion it.

Lord, I am not trying to make my way to your height, for my understanding is in no way equal to that. But I do desire to understand a little of your truth which my heart already believes and loves.

I do not seek to understand so that I can believe, but I believe so that I may understand. And what is more, I believe that unless I do believe, I shall not understand.

SAINT ANSELM (1033–1109)
Christian theologian and archbishop of Canterbury

PRAYERS
for
PEACE
and COMFORT

And the peace of God, which transcends all understanding, will guard your hearts and your minds in Christ Jesus.

PHILIPPIANS 4:7, NIV

The Serenity Prayer

God, grant me the serenity
To accept the things I cannot change,
Courage to change the things I can,
And wisdom to know the difference.
Living one day at a time,
Enjoying one moment at a time,
Accepting hardships as the pathway to peace,
Taking, as Jesus did,
This sinful world as it is,
Not as I would have it,
Trusting that you will make all things right,
If I surrender to your will,
So that I may be reasonably happy in this life,
And supremely happy with you
Forever in the next.
Amen.

REINHOLD NIEBUHR (1892–1971),
American pastor and theologian

I Need Thee

Lord, forgive me that when life's circumstances lift me
to the crest of the wave, I tend to forget Thee. Yet, like an
errant child, I have blamed Thee with my every failure,
even as I credit myself with every success.

When my fears evaporate like the morning mist, then
vainly I imagine that I am sufficient unto myself, that
material resources and human resources are enough.

I need Thee when the sun shines, lest I forget the storm and the dark. I need Thee when I am popular, when my friends and those who work beside me approve and compliment me. I need Thee more then, lest my head begin to swell.

O God, forgive me for my stupidity, my blindness in success, my lack of trust in Thee. Be Thou now my Savior in success.

Save me from conceit. Save me from pettiness. Save me from myself! And take this success, I pray, and use it for Thy glory. In Thy strength, I pray.

Amen.

Peter Marshall (1902–1949)
Pastor and chaplain of the United States Senate

The Shepherd's Psalm

The Lord is my shepherd, I lack nothing.

He makes me lie down in green pastures, he leads me beside quiet waters, he refreshes my soul.

He guides me along the right paths for his name's sake. Even though I walk through the darkest valley, I will fear no evil, for you are with me; your rod and your staff, they comfort me.

You prepare a table before me in the presence of my enemies. You anoint my head with oil; my cup overflows.

Surely your goodness and love will follow me all the days of my life, and I will dwell in the house of the Lord forever.

Psalm 23, NIV
A Psalm of David

For Dark Times

Almighty God:

Our sons, pride of our nation, this day have set upon a mighty endeavor, a struggle to preserve our Republic, our religion and our civilization, and to set free a suffering humanity.

Lead them straight and true; give strength to their arms, stoutness to their hearts, steadfastness in their faith. They will need Thy blessings. Their road will be long and hard. For the enemy is strong. He may hurl back our forces. Success may not come with rushing speed, but we shall return again and again; and we know by Thy grace, and by the righteousness of our cause, our sons will triumph.

Embrace these, Father, and receive them, Thy heroic servants, into Thy kingdom.

And for us at home—fathers, mothers, children, wives, sisters, and brothers of brave men overseas, whose thoughts and prayers are ever with them—help us, Almighty God, to rededicate ourselves in renewed faith in Thee in this hour of great sacrifice. Give us strength, too—strength in our daily tasks, to redouble the contributions we make in the physical and the material support of our armed forces.

With Thy blessing, we shall prevail over the unholy forces of our enemy. Help us to conquer the apostles of greed and racial arrogances. Lead us to the saving of our country, and with our sister nations into a world unity that will spell a sure peace—a peace invulnerable to the schemings of unworthy men. And a peace that will let

all men live in freedom, reaping the just rewards of their
honest toil.

FRANKLIN D. ROOSEVELT (1882–1945)
Thirty-second president of the United States of America
A PRAYER FROM D-DAY, JUNE 6, 1944

May I Be at Peace

May I be at peace.

May my heart remain open.

May I be aware of my true nature.

May I be healed.

May I be a source of healing to others.

May I dwell in the Breath of God.

SAINT TERESA OF AVILA (1515–1582)
Carmelite nun and mystic

Let Nothing Frighten You

Let nothing disturb you,

Let nothing frighten you,

All things are passing away:

God never changes.

Patience obtains all things

Whoever has God lacks nothing;

God alone suffices.

SAINT TERESA OF AVILA (1515–1582)
Carmelite nun and mystic

Joy Comes with Mourning

I will exalt you, Lord, for you rescued me. You refused to let my enemies triumph over me.

Lord my God, I cried to you for help, and you restored my health. You brought me up from the grave, O Lord. You kept me from falling into the pit of death.

Sing to the Lord, all you godly ones! Praise his holy name. For his anger lasts only a moment, but his favor lasts a lifetime! Weeping may last through the night, but joy comes with the morning.

When I was prosperous, I said, "Nothing can stop me now!" Your favor, O Lord, made me as secure as a mountain. Then you turned away from me, and I was shattered. I cried out to you, O Lord. I begged the Lord for mercy, saying, "What will you gain if I die, if I sink into the grave? Can my dust praise you? Can it tell of your faithfulness? Hear me, Lord, and have mercy on me. Help me, O Lord."

You have turned my mourning into joyful dancing. You have taken away my clothes of mourning and clothed me with joy, that I might sing praises to you and not be silent.

O Lord my God, I will give you thanks forever!

Psalm 30, NLT

No More Worry

I find my happiness, my delight, my fulfillment, my joy in You, oh Lord.

I will express a kind, calm, gentle, affirming spirit in every situation and to everyone I meet. Because You are near to me, Lord. If I start to worry or become afraid, please remind me, and help me to remind myself You are always present—next to me, inside of me.

So I'm not gong to worry about anything in life big or small. You are with me. And You invite me to bring any concerns, questions, fears, and worries to You and You will give me a peace that is above anything I can hope or imagine or do for myself.

Thank You so much. Thank You for guarding my heart and mind from worry and stress.

I believe in You and Your goodness, oh Lord. My heart and mind are focused on You. I'm not going to get dragged down by the corruption of the world, but will keep my eyes on things that are good, noble, holy, pure, and beautiful. I will walk confidently and boldly in Your will and ways.

I pray that my spirit and conduct will be a light that shows others who You are and just how good and loving You are.

Amen.

MARK GILROY (b. 1958)
A first-person paraphrase of Philippians 4:4–8

Father of All Mercy

All praise to the God and Father of our Master, Jesus the Messiah! Father of all mercy! God of all healing counsel! He comes alongside us when we go through hard times, and before you know it, he brings us alongside someone else who is going through hard times so that we can be

there for that person just as God was there for us. We have
plenty of hard times that come from following the Messiah,
but no more so than the good times of his healing comfort—
we get a full measure of that, too.

2 Corinthians 1:3–5
The Message

For the Grieving

O Merciful God, and heavenly Father, who has taught us in
your holy Word that you do not willingly afflict or grieve
your children; look with pity, we beseech you, upon the
sorrows of your servant for whom our prayers are offered.

Remember him, O Lord, in mercy; fill his soul with
patience; comfort him with a sense of your goodness; lift up
your countenance upon him, and give him peace; through
Jesus Christ our Lord.

Amen.

Adapted from *The Book of Common Prayer*

All Our Strivings Cease

Drop Thy still dews of quietness,
Till all our strivings cease;
Take from our souls the strain and stress,
And let our ordered lives confess
The beauty of Thy peace.

JOHN GREENLEAF WHITTIER (1807–1892)
American Quaker poet

It Is Well with My Soul

When peace, like a river, attendeth my way,
When sorrows like sea billows roll;
Whatever my lot, Thou has taught me to say,
It is well, it is well, with my soul.

Though Satan should buffet, though trials should come,
Let this blest assurance control,
That Christ has regarded my helpless estate,
And hath shed His own blood for my soul.

My sin, oh, the bliss of this glorious thought!
My sin, not in part but the whole,
Is nailed to the cross, and I bear it no more,
Praise the Lord, praise the Lord, O my soul!

And Lord, haste the day when my faith shall be sight,
The clouds be rolled back as a scroll;
The trump shall resound, and the Lord shall descend,
Even so, it is well with my soul.

It is well, with my soul,
It is well, with my soul,
It is well, it is well, with my soul.

HORATIO SPAFFORD (1828–1888)
American businessman

PRAYERS
of
PETITION

And my God will meet all your needs
according to the riches of his glory in
Christ Jesus.

PHILIPPIANS 4:19, NIV

A Prayer to Enjoy Life
(Prayer of a Confederate Soldier)

I asked God for strength, that I might achieve; I was made weak, that I might learn humbly to obey.

I asked for health, that I might do greater things; I was given infirmity, that I might do better things.

I asked for riches, that I might be happy; I was given poverty, that I might be wise.

I asked for power, that I might have the praise of men; I was given weakness, that I might feel the need of God.

I asked for all things, that I might enjoy life; I was given life, that I might enjoy all things.

I got nothing that I asked for, but everything I hoped for. Almost despite myself, my unspoken prayers were answered.

I am among all men most richly blessed.

AUTHOR UNKNOWN
Attributed to a Confederate soldier
toward the end of the Civil War

A Prayer for Rest

O Lord God, who hast given man the night for rest, as thou hast created the day in which he may employ himself in labor, grant, I pray, that my body may so rest during this night that my mind cease not to be awake to thee, nor my heart faint or be overcome with torpor, preventing it from adhering steadfastly to the love of thee. While laying aside my cares to relax and relieve my mind, may I not, in the meanwhile, forget thee, nor may the remembrance of thy goodness and grace, which ought always to be deeply engraved on my mind, escape my memory.

In like manner, also, as the body rests may my conscience enjoy rest. Grant, moreover, that in taking sleep I may not give indulgence to the flesh, but only allow myself as much as the weakness of this natural state requires, to my being enabled thereafter to be more alert in thy service. Be pleased to keep me so chaste and unpolluted, not less in mind than in body, and safe from all dangers that my sleep itself may turn to the glory of thy name.

But since this day has not passed away without my having in many ways offended thee through my proneness to evil, in like manner as all things are now covered by the darkness of the night, so let every thing that is sinful in me lie buried in thy mercy. Hear me, O God, Father and Preserver, through Jesus Christ thy Son. Amen.

JOHN CALVIN (1509–1564)
Theologian of the Protestant Reformation

A Prayer for Courage

Dear God,

With You on my side, I know in my mind that I have absolutely nothing to fear. But I still have a fear in my heart. There are times when I take my eyes off You—when I forget Your promise that You will never leave me nor forsake me— and I let fear invade and take control of my life.

Right now I feel defeated by fear. I am not doing what I am supposed to in life because I am afraid of what will happen to me. I am struggling to trust You to protect and empower me. My eyes are focused on what I perceive to be threats all around me, rather than focused on You. Even before I speak it, You know the specific fear that is most plaguing my life right now.

God, I ask that You do a work in my heart and my mind that I cannot do myself. Please remove the fear that is robbing me of joy, purpose, and success. Help me to trust You as the one true source of courage. I don't claim courage through my own strength, but I do receive the courage I need for the challenges and tasks facing me because I trust You and I know You love me.

I affirm Your promise that You will never leave me nor forsake me. Thank You for the courage that comes from that trust.

In Your Mighty Name,
Amen.

MARK GILROY (1958–)
From *God's Help for Your Every Need*
Used with permission

Your Healing Hand

Sacred Heart of Jesus, you invite all who are heavy burdened to come to you and find rest.

Teach me to reach out to you in my need;
Teach me to lead others to your Sacred Heart;
Teach me with your compassion for others;
Teach me with your courage and love for all;
Teach me with your wisdom and grace;

Touch gently my life with your healing hand.

Amen.

JOHN PREDMORE (1961–)
Jesuit priest and pastor in Amman, Jordan

Give Me Faith

If e'er thine ear in mercy bent,
When wretched mortals cried to Thee,
And if, indeed, Thy Son was sent,
To save lost sinners such as me:

Then hear me now, while, kneeling here,
I lift to Thee my heart and eye,
And all my soul ascends in prayer,
Oh, give me—give me Faith! I cry.

Without some glimmering in my heart,
I could not raise this fervent prayer;
But, oh! a stronger light impart,
And in Thy mercy fix it there.

While Faith is with me, I am blest;
It turns my darkest night to day;
But while I clasp it to my breast,
I often feel it slide away.

Then, cold and dark, my spirit sinks,
To see my light of life depart;
And every fiend of Hell, methinks,
Enjoys the anguish of my heart.

What shall I do, if all my love,
My hopes, my toil, are cast away,
And if there be no God above,
To hear and bless me when I pray?

If this be vain delusion all,
If death be an eternal sleep,
And none can hear my secret call,
Or see the silent tears I weep!

Oh, help me, God! For Thou alone
Canst my distracted soul relieve;
Forsake it not: it is Thine own,
Though weak, yet longing to believe.

Oh, drive these cruel doubts away;
And make me know, that Thou art God!
A Faith, that shines by night and day,
Will lighten every earthly load.

If I believe that Jesus died,
And, waking, rose to reign above;
Then surely Sorrow, Sin, and Pride,
Must yield to Peace, and Hope, and Love.

And all the blessed words He said
Will strength and holy joy impart:
A shield of safety o'er my head,
A spring of comfort in my heart.

G. K. CHESTERTON (1874–1936)
British philosopher, author, and critic
Excerpt from "A Prayer in Darkness"

A Prayer for Success
(The Prayer of Jabez)

Oh, that You would bless me indeed, and enlarge my territory, that Your hand would be with me, and that YOU would keep me from evil, that I may not cause pain!

1 Chronicles 4:10, NKJV

A Prayer for Raising Children

Almighty God, heavenly Father, you have blessed us with the joy and care of children: Give us calm strength and patient wisdom as we bring them up, that we may teach them to love whatever is just and true and good, following the example of our Savior Jesus Christ. Amen.

From *The Book of Common Book Prayer*

A Prayer for Guidance

O eternal and everlasting God, I presume to present myself this morning before thy Divine majesty, beseeching thee to accept of my humble and hearty thanks, that it hath pleased thy great goodness to keep and preserve me the night past from all the dangers poor mortals are subject to, and has given me sweet and pleasant sleep, whereby I find my body refreshed and comforted for performing the duties of this day, in which I beseech thee to defend me from all perils of body and soul.

Increase my faith in the sweet promises of the gospel; give me repentance from dead works; pardon my wanderings, and direct my thoughts unto thyself, the

God of my salvation; teach me how to live in thy fear, labor in thy service, and ever to run in the ways of thy commandments; make me always watchful over my heart, that neither the terrors of conscience, the loathing of holy duties, the love of sin, nor an unwillingness to depart this life, may cast me into a spiritual slumber, but daily frame me more and more into the likeness of thy son Jesus Christ, that living in thy fear, and dying in thy favor, I may in thy appointed time attain the resurrection of the just unto eternal life bless my family, friends, and kindred.

GEORGE WASHINGTON (1732–1799)
First president of the United States of America

To Grow Old Gracefully

Lord, you know better than I know myself that I am growing older and one day will be old.

Keep me from the fatal habit of thinking I must say something on every subject and on every occasion.

Release me from craving to straighten out everybody's affairs.

Make me thoughtful but not moody; helpful but not bossy.

With my vast store of wisdom it seems a pity not to use it all; but you know, Lord, that I want a few friends at the end.

Keep my mind free from the recital of endless details, give me wings to get to the point.

Seal my lips on my aches and pains, they are increasing and love of rehearsing them is becoming sweeter as the years go by.

I dare not ask for grace enough to enjoy the tales of other's pains, but help me to endure them with patience.

I dare not ask for improved memory, but for growing humility and a lessening cocksureness when my memory seems to clash with the memories of others.

Teach me the glorious lesson that occasionally I may be mistaken.

Keep me reasonably sweet; I do not want to be a saint, some of them are so hard to live with, but a sour old person is one of the crowning works of the devil.

Give me the ability to see good things in unexpected places and talent in unexpected people, and give me O Lord the grace to tell them so.

Amen.

Anonymous Nun
Seventeenth century

A Prayer for Patience

Lord, who hast suffer'd all for me,
My peace and pardon to procure,
The lighter cross I bear for Thee,
Help me with patience to endure.

The storm of loud repining hush;
I would in humble silence mourn;
Why should the unburnt, though burning bush,
Be angry as the crackling thorn?

Man should not faint at Thy rebuke,
Like Joshua falling on his face,
When the cursed thing that Achan took
Brought Israel into just disgrace.

Perhaps some golden wedge suppress'd,
Some secret sin offends my God;
Perhaps that Babylonish vest,
Self-righteousness, provokes the rod.

Ah! were I buffeted all day,
Mock'd, crown'd with thorns and spit upon,
I yet should have no right to say,
My great distress is mine alone.

Let me not angrily declare
No pain was ever sharp like mine,
Nor murmur at the cross I bear,
But rather weep, remembering Thine.

WILLIAM COWPER (1731–1800)
English poet and hymnist

A Prayer for Family

Lord, we thank you for this day
For the many gifts you have heaped on us
For the laughter and wonder of these young hearts
Who share our days and our nights
For sun and rain and growing things

Gifts of companionship
Watch over this family Lord,
See us through our challenges
Mark the days of our lives, this moment, this week
With joys too great to measure
Lives rich in your good grace
Your love, your guidance
Unburden our hearts, relieve our pain
Still our quiet, our fears
Bless us Lord in the busy week to come

RAYMOND A. FOSS (1960–)
American poet

A Prayer for Job Promotion

Dear Heavenly Father,

When so many people are out of work I am grateful
that You have blessed me with the means to a livelihood.
I know that with a roof over my head and food on the
table I already live better than many in the world.

So it is with a sense of gratitude for all I already have
and have been given that I come to You with the request
for promotion. I truly believe You have planted in my
heart the desire to grow in my skills, to assume greater
responsibilities, to exercise leadership to a greater degree
in ways that helps others to grow.

I pray first of all that You would help me to walk worthy
of a promotion. Reveal in my heart and spirit ways that
I need to grow and personally improve to be ready for

promotion. I pray that You will bless my work and influence and that all I do will positively contribute to the growth of my company and the workers around me. I pray that You will bring me and my work to the attention of those in positions to offer promotion.

But I affirm that promotion ultimately comes from You and I will not forget to thank and praise You for Your work on my behalf.

In the Name of the Lord,
Amen.

MARK GILROY (1958–)
From *God's Help for Your Every Need*
Used with permission.

PRAYERS

-> *of* <-

DEVOTION

Love the Lord your God with all your
heart and with all your soul and with
all your strength.

DEUTERONOMY 6:5, NIV

The Whole of Myself

Lord, because you have made me, I owe you the whole of my love;

Because you have redeemed me, I owe you the whole of myself;

Because you have promised so much, I owe you my whole being.

I owe you much more love than I owe to myself, as you are greater than I, for whom you gave yourself and to whom you promised yourself.

I pray you, Lord, make me taste by love what I taste by knowledge; let me know by love what I know by understanding.

I owe you more than my whole self, but I have no more, and by myself I cannot render the whole of it to you.

Draw me to you, Lord, in the fullness of your love. I am wholly yours by creation; make me all yours, too, in love.

Saint Anselm (1033–1109)
Christian theologian and archbishop of Canterbury

My Desire to Please You

My Lord God, I have no idea where I am going. I do not see the road ahead of me. I cannot know for certain where it will end. Nor do I really know myself, and the fact that I think I am following Your will does not mean that I am actually doing so. But I believe that the desire to please You does in fact please You.

And I hope I have that desire in all that I am doing. I hope that I will never do anything apart from that desire.

And I know that, if I do this, You will lead me by the right road, though I may know nothing about it.

Therefore I will trust You always though I may seem to be lost and in the shadow of death. I will not fear, for You are ever with me, and You will never leave me to face my perils alone.

THOMAS MERTON (1915–1968)
Trappist monk and Catholic writer

The Covenant Prayer

I am no longer my own, but thine.
Put me to what thou wilt, rank me with whom thou wilt.
Put me to doing, put me to suffering.
Let me be employed for thee or laid aside for thee, exalted
    for thee or brought low for thee.
Let me be full, let me be empty.
Let me have all things, let me have nothing.
I freely and heartily yield all things to thy pleasure and
    disposal.
And now, O glorious and blessed God, Father, Son and Holy
    Spirit, thou art mine, and I am thine.
So be it.
And the covenant which I have made on earth, let it be
    ratified in heaven.
Amen.

JOHN WESLEY (1703–1791)
Anglican cleric, reformer and
father of the Methodist Movement

A Prayer to Live as We Ought

Lord, get us up above the world. Come, Holy Spirit, heavenly Dove, and mount and bear us on Your wings, far from these inferior sorrows and inferior joys, up where eternal ages roll. May we ascend in joyful contemplation, and may our spirit come back again, strong for all its service, armed for all its battles, armored for all its dangers, and made ready to live heaven on earth until soon we shall live heaven in heaven.

Great Father, be with Your waiting people: any in great trouble please greatly help; any that are despondent sweetly comfort and cheer; any that have erred and are smarting under their own sin, bring them back and heal their wounds; any that are panting after holiness give them the desire of their hearts; any that are longing for usefulness lead them in ways of usefulness.

Lord, we want to live while we live. We do pray that we may not merely groan out an existence here below, nor live as earthworms crawling back in our holes and dragging now and then a withered leaf with us; but Oh! give us to live as we ought to live, with a new life that You have put in us, with the divine quickening which has lifted us as much above common men as men are lifted above the beasts that perish.

Do not let us always be hampered like poor half-hatched birds within the egg; may we chip the shell today and get out in the glorious liberty of the children of God. Grant us this, we pray You.

CHARLES H. SPURGEON (1834–1892)
British Baptist preacher and author

Fill Us with Holy Love

Look upon us, O Lord, and let all the darkness of our souls vanish before the beams of thy brightness.

Fill us with holy love, and open to us the treasures of thy wisdom.

All our desire is known unto thee, therefore perfect what thou hast begun, and what thy Spirit has awakened us to ask in prayer.

We seek thy face, turn thy face unto us and show us thy glory.

Then shall our longing be satisfied, and our peace shall be perfect.

SAINT AUGUSTINE (354–430)
Christian theologian and philosopher

Knowing Christ Jesus

But whatever were gains to me I now consider loss for the sake of Christ. What is more, I consider everything a loss because of the surpassing worth of knowing Christ Jesus my Lord, for whose sake I have lost all things. I consider them garbage, that I may gain Christ and be found in him, not having a righteousness of my own that comes from the law, but that which is through faith in Christ—the righteousness that comes from God on the basis of faith.

I want to know Christ—yes, to know the power of his resurrection and participation in his sufferings, becoming like him in his death, and so, somehow, attaining to the resurrection from the dead.

Not that I have already obtained all this, or have already arrived at my goal, but I press on to take hold of that for which Christ Jesus took hold of me.

Brothers and sisters, I do not consider myself yet to have taken hold of it. But one thing I do: Forgetting what is behind and straining toward what is ahead, I press on toward the goal to win the prize for which God has called me heavenward in Christ Jesus.

Philippians 3:7–14, NIV

I Long for Your Companionship

Jesus, my feet are dirty. Come even as a slave to me, pour water into your bowl, come and wash my feet. In asking such a thing I know I am overbold, but I dread what was threatened when you said to me, "If I do not wash your feet I have no fellowship with you." Wash my feet then, because I long for your companionship.

SAINT ORIGEN (182–254)
Early Christian theologian

Let Thy Will Be Done

What Conscience dictates to be done,
Or warns me not to do;
This teach me more than Hell to shun,
That more than Heav'n pursue.

What blessings thy free bounty gives
Let me not cast away;
For God is paid when man receives;
T' enjoy is to obey.

Let not this weak, unknowing hand
Presume thy bolts to throw,
And teach damnation round the land
On each I judge thy foe.

If I am right, thy grace impart,
Still in the right to stay;
If I am wrong, O teach my heart
To find that better way.

Save me alike from foolish Pride
Or impious Discontent,
At aught thy wisdom has denied,
Or aught that goodness lent.

Teach me to feel another's woe,
To right the fault I see:
That mercy I to others show,
That mercy show to me.

This day be bread and peace my lot:
All else beneath the sun
Though know'st if best bestow'd or not,
And let Thy will be done.

To Thee, whose temple is of Space,
Whose altar earth, sea, skies,
One chorus let all Beings raise!
All Nature's incense rise!

ALEXANDER POPE (1688–1744)
English poet and satirist

A Spirit to Know You

Gracious and Holy Father,

Please give me: intellect to understand you, reason to discern you, diligence to seek you, wisdom to find you, a spirit to know you, a heart to meditate upon you, ears to hear you, eyes to see you, a tongue to proclaim you, a way of life pleasing to you, patience to wait for you, and perseverance to look for you.

Grant me a perfect end, your holy presence, a blessed resurrection, and life everlasting.

Amen.

SAINT BENEDICT (480–543)
Patron saint of Europe and students

Unworthy to Be, but Accepted in Thee

Dear Lord Jesus, we're unworthy to be members of Thy church, but we are not dominated by the devil into letting our unworthiness make us morbidly unbelieving. Even though we're not worthy to be, we're accepted in Thee.

Thou hast made us members of Thy body, and we accept it, and we leave the matter of our work with Thee. If angels or archangels question our right to be there, we look to Thee as a sheep looks to his shepherd and say, "Answer for me Lord, answer for me. I admit I am not worthy, but answer for me dear Lord." And Thou wilt answer for us for Thou didst come from high heaven to low earth, from the immortal and eternal liberty of the Godhead to the confines of the virgin's womb, that we might be redeemed.

Thou didst die on the cross of shame and suffering and rise that we might be justified and forgiven, and you reunited again with the Father from which we fell in the fall. God all this is true and we leave it with Thee.

All this we pray in Christ's name.

Amen.

A.W. TOZER (1897–1963)
American pastor, author, and magazine editor

A Martyr's Prayer

I am the wheat of God, and am ground by the teeth of the wild beasts, that I may be found the pure bread of God.

I long after the Lord, the Son of the true God and Father, Jesus Christ. Him I seek, who died for us and rose again. I am eager to die for the sake of Christ. My love has been crucified, and there is no fire in me that loves anything.

But there is living water springing up in me, and it says to me inwardly: "Come to the Father."

SAINT IGNATIUS (50–117)
Bishop of Antioch

Christ Be with Me

Christ with me, Christ before me, Christ behind me,
Christ in me, Christ beneath me, Christ above me,
Christ on my right, Christ on my left,
Christ where I lie, Christ where I sit, Christ where I arise,
Christ in the heart of everyone who thinks of me,

Christ in the mouth of every one who speaks to me,
Christ in every eye that sees me,
Christ in every ear that hears me.
Salvation is of the Lord.
Salvation is of the Christ.
May your salvation, Lord, be ever with us.

SAINT PATRICK (387–late fifth century)
Patron saint of Ireland

To Love Thee More Dearly

Thanks be to thee, my Lord Jesus Christ,
For all the benefits thou hast won for me,
For all the pains and insults thou hast borne for me.
O most merciful Redeemer, Friend, and Brother,
May I know thee more clearly,
Love thee more dearly,
And follow thee more nearly,
For ever and ever.

RICHARD DE WYCH (1197–1253)
Bishop of Chichester

PRAYERS

of

SERVICE

For even the Son of Man came not to be
served but to serve others and to give
his life as a ransom for many.

MARK 10:45, NLT

Make Me an Instrument of Your Peace

Lord, make me an instrument of your peace.
Where there is hatred, let me sow love,
Where there is injury, pardon,
Where there is doubt, faith,
Where there is despair, hope,
Where there is darkness, light,
Where there is sadness, joy.

O Divine Master, grant that I may
Not so much seek to be consoled as to console,
Not so much to be understood as to understand,
Not so much to be loved, as to love;
Nor it is in giving that we receive,
It is in pardoning that we are pardoned,
It is in dying that we awake to eternal life.

SAINT FRANCIS OF ASSISI (d. 1226)
Patron saint of animals and nature

A Faithful Steward

Almighty God, whose loving hand hath given us all that
we possess: Grant us grace that we may honor thee with
our substance, and, remembering the account which we
must one day give, may be faithful stewards of thy bounty,
through Jesus Christ our Lord.

Amen.

From *The Book of Common Prayer*

The World Is Better That I Lived

Let me today do something that shall take
A little sadness from the world's vast store,
And may I be so favored as to make
Of joy's too scanty sum a little more.

Let me not hurt, by any selfish deed
Or thoughtless word, the heart of foe or friend;
Nor would I pass, unseeing, worthy need,
Or sin by silence when I should defend.

However meager be my worldly wealth,
Let me give something that shall aid my kind—
A word of courage, or a thought of health,
Dropped as I pass for troubled hearts to find.

Let me to-night look back across the span
'Twixt dawn and dark, and to my conscience say—
Because of some good act to beast or man—
"The world is better that I lived today."

ELLA WHEELER WILCOX (1850–1919)
American author and poet

A Prayer for Serving Others

Father,
Allow me to serve others with a joyful heart;
Never keeping score;
Always giving;
Never expecting to receive.

Allow me to give of myself,
To give of my talents and of my goods,
To give of my time and of my energy,
To give of my heart and of my soul.
Help me understand the needs of others,
Never criticizing,
Never demeaning,
Never scolding,
Never condemning.

You have been so gracious to me,
Always loving,
Always forgiving,
Always restoring;
Never gloating over my defeats,
Even when I have been so wrong.

Father, keep a condemning spirit
Far from my heart and further from my lips.
Allow me to serve others as You serve,
With gentleness, compassion, and tenderness,
Never diminishing the worth of another,
Choosing to extend mercy to the brokenhearted,
Like You have repeatedly shown it to me.

JACK WATTS (1956–)
American author

That All May Know

Everliving God, whose will it is that all should come to you through your Son Jesus Christ: Inspire our witness to him, that all may know the power of his forgiveness and the hope of his resurrection; who lives and reigns with you and the Holy Spirit, one God, now and for ever.

Amen.

From The Book of Common Prayer

Shining on Through Us

Dear Jesus,

Help us to spread your fragrance everywhere we go, flood our souls with your spirit and life. Penetrate and possess our whole being so utterly that our lives may only be a radiance of yours. Shine through us and be so in us that every soul we come in contact with may feel your presence in our soul. Let them look up and see no longer us but only Jesus. Stay with us and then we shall begin to shine as you shine, so to shine as to be light to others.

The light, O Jesus, will be all from you. None of it will be ours. It will be your shining on others through us.

Let us thus praise you in the way you love best by shining on those around us. Let us preach you without preaching not by words, but by our example by the catching force the sympathetic influence of what we do the evident fullness of the love our hearts bear to you.

MOTHER TERESA OF CALCUTTA (1910–1997)
Catholic religious sister and missionary

To Help People

Heavenly Father, we bow our heads and thank You for Your love. Accept our thanks for the peace that yields this day and the shared faith that makes its continuance likely.

Make us strong to do Your work, willing to heed and hear Your will, and write on our hearts these words: "Use power to help people."

For we are given power not to advance our own purposes, nor to make a great show in the world, nor a name. There is but one just use of power, and it is to serve people. Help us to remember it, Lord.

The Lord our God be with us, as He was with our fathers; may He not leave us or forsake us; so that He may incline our hearts to Him, to walk in all His ways that all peoples of the earth may know that the Lord is God; there is no other.

GEORGE H. W. BUSH (1924–)
Forty-first president of the United States of America
Excerpted from inaugural address, January 20, 1989

A Prayer to Be a Blessing

Merciful God,

You are an awesome God, full of compassion and kindness. Your love and mercy know no bounds. Your heart is always turned toward those who are hurting and who have serious needs. You are the father of the orphan and the husband of the widow. You give sight to the blind. You have a special place in your heart for the poor.

I want to do good deeds and help others. I know that my family needs me. But I also know how much it pleases you when I reach out to others who are in need. I ask that you renew in me a heart of compassion and give me the strength to do something about it.

As I share with the needy with both my finances and my time, I will remember to praise you for the many blessings you have given me. Open my eyes to the need around the world—and across the street.

In Jesus' name,

Amen.

MARK GILROY (1958–)
From *God's Help for Your Every Need*
Used with permission

Confession

Lord, I have sinned in all the branches of sloth; by my negligence I have been slow in God's service, slothful and negligent in the faith, and I have taken great care and thought for the ease of my vile body, and I have not remembered the words of the Scriptures, nor followed after them, by reason of my sloth. Again I have not given thanks to God, as I should, for the spiritual and temporal blessings that He has given and sent me, and furthermore I have not served God as I ought, according to the blessings and virtues that He has given me. I have neither said nor done those good things which I might has said or done, and I have been slow and slothful in the service of Our Lord,

and have done and busied myself in the service of worldly
things, and also I have better served myself and mine own
flesh and have set more store thereby, than in the service of
my sweet Creator. I have long been full idle, whence many
evils and ill thoughts and meditations be come to me.

A CITIZEN OF PARIS, c.1393
From *The Goodman of Paris:
A Treatise on Moral and Domestic Economy*

To Serve Others

O Lord our heavenly Father, whose blessed Son came not to
be served but to serve:

Bless, we beseech thee, all who, following in his steps,
give themselves to the service of others; that with wisdom,
patience, and courage, they may minister in his name to the
suffering, the friendless, and the needy; for the love of him
who laid down his life for us, the same thy Son our Savior
Jesus Christ, who liveth and reigneth with thee and the
Holy Spirit, one God, for ever and ever.

Amen.

ANONYMOUS

A Prayer for a Meaningful Life

I would like to have my frequent prayer answered that
God let my life be meaningful in the enhancement of His
kingdom and that my life might be meaningful in the
enhancement of the lives of my fellow human beings.

I call upon all the people of our Nation to give thanks on that day for the blessings Almighty God has bestowed upon us, and to join the fervent prayer of George Washington who as President asked God to "impart all the blessings we possess, or ask for ourselves to the whole family of mankind."

JIMMY CARTER (1924–)
Thirty-ninth president of the United States of America

Lord, make my life
A window for Your light
To shine through
And a mirror to reflect Your love
To all I meet.
Amen.

ROBERT SCHULLER (1926–)
American pastor, author, and motivational speaker

PRAYERS
of
BLESSING

Now may the God of hope fill you with all joy and peace in believing, that you may abound in hope by the power of the Holy Spirit.

ROMANS 15:13, NKJV

May the Lord Bless You

May the Lord bless you and protect you.

May the Lord smile on you and be gracious to you.

May the Lord show you his favor and give you his peace.

Numbers 6:24–26, NLT

We Praise You

For your goodness and generosity
In giving us all we need,
Help us to praise you O God.

In every circumstance of life,
In good times and bad,
Help us to trust you, O God.

In love and faithfulness,
With all that we have and all that we are,
Help us to serve you, O God.

As we speak or write or listen
To those nearby or far away,
Help us to share your love, O God.

In our plans and work
For ourselves and for others,
Help us to glorify you, O God.

In every thought and word and deed,
By the power of your Holy Spirit,
This week, may we live for you, O God.

Church of Australia, Contemporary Liturgy

United in Love

O Sovereign and almighty Lord, bless all your people, and all your flock. Give your peace, your help, your love unto us your servants, the sheep of your fold, that we may be united in the bond of peace and love, one body and one spirit, in one hope of our calling, in your divine and boundless love.

Liturgy of Saint Mark, used by the
Orthodox Church of Alexandria, fourth century

An Irish Blessing

May the blessing of light be on you—light without and light within. May the blessed sunlight shine on you and warm your heart till it glows like a great peat fire, so that the stranger may come and warm himself at it, and also a friend. And may the light shine out of the two eyes of you, like a candle set in two windows of a house, bidding the wanderer to come in out of the storm.

And may the blessing of the rain be on you—the soft sweet rain. May it fall upon your spirit so that all the little flowers may spring up, and shed their sweetness on the air. And may the blessing of the great rains be on you, may they beat upon your spirit and wash it fair and clean, and leave there many a shining pool where the blue of heaven shines, and sometimes a star.

And may the blessing of the earth be on you—the great round earth; may you ever have a kindly greeting for them you pass as you're going along the roads. May the earth be soft under you when you rest upon it, tired at the end of the day, and may it rest easy over you when, at the last, you lay out under it; may it rest so lightly over you, that your soul may be out from under it quickly, and up, and off, and on its way to God.

May the road rise to meet you. May the wind be always at your back. May the sun shine warm upon your face, and the rains fall soft upon your fields.

And until we meet again may God hold you in the palm of his hand.

Traditional

We Bless You God

O Lord God Almighty, Father of angels and men, we praise and bless your holy name for all your goodness and loving kindness to humanity.

We bless you for our creation, preservation, and for your unceasing generosity to us throughout our lives.

But above all, we bless you for your great love in the redemption of the world by our Lord Jesus Christ.

We bless you for bringing us safe to the beginning of a new day. Grant that this day we fall into no sin, neither run into any kind of danger.

Keep us, we pray, from all things hurtful to body or soul, and grant us your pardon and peace, so that, being cleansed from all our sins, we might serve you with quiet hearts and minds, and continue in the same until our life's end, through Jesus Christ, our Savior and Redeemer.

JOHN WESLEY (1703–1791)
British evangelist, author, reformer, and father of
the Methodist Movement

The Traveler's Psalm

I lift up my eyes to the mountains—where does my help come from?

My help comes from the Lord, the Maker of heaven and earth.

He will not let your foot slip—he who watches over you will not slumber; indeed, he who watches over Israel will neither slumber nor sleep.

The Lord watches over you—the Lord is your shade at your right hand; the sun will not harm you by day, nor the moon by night.

The Lord will keep you from all harm—he will watch over your life; the Lord will watch over your coming and going both now and forevermore.

Psalm 121, NIV

Bless This Nation

O Lord our Heavenly Father, high and mighty King of kings, and Lord of lords, who dost from your throne behold all the dwellers on earth and reignest with power supreme and uncontrolled over all the Kingdoms, Empires and Governments; look down in mercy, we beseech Thee, on these our American States, who have fled to Thee from the rod of the oppressor and thrown themselves on Your gracious protection, desiring to be henceforth dependent only on Thee.

To Thee have they appealed for the righteousness of their cause; to Thee do they now look up for that countenance and support, which Thou alone canst give.

Take them, therefore, Heavenly Father, under Your nurturing care; give them wisdom in Council and valor in the field; defeat the malicious designs of our cruel adversaries; convince them of the unrighteousness of their Cause and if they persist in their sanguinary purposes, O, let the voice of Thy own unerring justice, sounding in their hearts, constrain them to drop the weapons of war from their unnerved hands in the day of battle!

Be Thou present, O God of wisdom, and direct the councils of this honorable assembly; enable them to settle things on the best and surest foundation. That the scene of blood may be speedily closed; that order, harmony and peace may be effectually restored, and truth and justice, religion and piety, prevail and flourish amongst the people. Preserve the health of their bodies and vigor of their minds; shower down on them and the millions they here represent, such temporal blessings as Thou seest expedient for them in this world and crown them with everlasting glory in the world to come.

All this we ask in the name and through the merits of Jesus Christ, Your Son and our Savior.

Amen.

REVEREND JACOB DUCHÉ (1737–1798)
Rector of Christ Church of Philadelphia
First prayer of the Continental Congress, 1774

A Blessing to Forget— and to Remember

Always remember to forget the things that made you sad.
But never forget to remember the things that made you glad.
Always remember to forget the friends that proved untrue.
But never forget to remember those that have stuck by you.
Always remember to forget the troubles that passed away.
But never forget to remember the blessings that come
each day.

Traditional Irish blessing

Blessing for Youth

Almighty God,

We ask your blessing upon our young people gathered here. You have gifted each one of them in a special and unique way. May they come to know and share the wonder and awe that lives within them as they grow in wisdom, knowledge and understanding of you.

Guide and sustain them as they discern your invitation to discipleship.

Bless their openness and enthusiasm and allow their questions to both enliven and challenge us as a community of believers gathered to do your will.

Strengthen and support the many good works they do. Challenge and provoke them along their journey of faith so they may help lead the church into the possibilities of tomorrow.

In all these things, we ask your blessing upon them this day, in the name of the Father, the Son and the Holy Spirit. Amen.

A Prayer for World Youth Day

Scriptural Blessing for Youth

The Lord created you just the way you are, inside and outside. He formed and shaped you when you were still in your mother's womb. He designed you with a special purpose. You are wonderful just the way you are. And never forget. God has incredible plans for your life. Plans for success, not failure . . . plans to fill you with hope and excitement for your future.

Paraphrased from Psalm 139:13–14
and Jeremiah 29:11

A Blessing for Parents

Almighty God, You know what it is like to be both Mother and Father to us all.

We ask You, the source and sustainer of all life, to bless these parents in the role you have set before them.

Gift their lips with the wisdom to speak the truth so it can be heard.

Gift their ears with sensitivity as they listen to the needs of their children.

Gift their souls with a faith radiating your intimate presence in their life.

Gift their minds with patience and understanding to handle the changing needs and demands placed before them each day.

Guide their hearts as they seek out and reconcile the areas of conflict and pain that may exist.

And through all these things, may your abundant blessings continue to affirm and support all they do as parents.

We ask this blessing upon each of them, in the name of the Father, the Son and the Holy Spirit.

Amen.

A Prayer for World Youth Day

A Blessing for Grandparents

Lord Jesus, you were born of the Virgin Mary, the daughter of Saints Joachim and Anne.

Look with love on grandparents the world over. Protect them! They are a source of enrichment for families, for the Church and for all of society.

Support them! As they grow older, may they continue to be for their families strong pillars of Gospel faith, guardian of noble domestic ideals, living treasures of sound religious traditions.

Make them teachers of wisdom and courage, that they may pass on to future generations the fruits of their mature human and spiritual experience.

Lord Jesus, help families and society to value the presence and roles of grandparents. May they never be ignored or excluded, but always encounter respect and love.

Help them to live serenely and to feel welcomed in all the years of life which you give them.

Mary, Mother of all the living, keep grandparents constantly in your care, accompany them on their earthly pilgrimage, and by your prayers, grant that all families may one day be reunited in our heavenly homeland, where you await all humanity for the great embrace of live without end.

Amen.

POPE BENEDICT XVI (1927–)

Enlighten Us

May God the Father bless us; may Christ take care of us; the Holy Ghost enlighten us all the days of our life.

The Lord be our defender and keeper of body and soul, both now and for ever, to the ages of ages.

SAINT AETHELWOLD (d. 984)
Bishop of Winchester and monastic reformer

PRAYERS

_of_

INTERCESSION

I urge, then, first of all, that petitions,
prayers, intercession and thanksgiving
be made for all people.

1 Timothy 2:1, NKJV

For All Who Struggle

For continuing or renewed health for all those I love—
Strengthen them in your mercy, Lord.

For all struggling with life-threatening illness—Be their
source of comfort, O Good Shepherd.

For all weakened by age or infirmity—Strengthen both
their limbs and their spirit, O God.

For all suffering from mental or nervous afflictions—
Be their calming presence, Lord Jesus.

For all with disabling handicaps—Give them courage
and patience, O Lord.

For all struggling with spiritual anxiety, depression or
addiction—Shower them with your love and mercy, O God.

For all who feel alone, for the lonely, the marginalized,
the homebound, the shunned, and those who feel on the
edge of society—Let them feel your comforting presence.

For all close to death—Ease their pain and grant them
your peace, O Sacred Heart.

For doctors, nurses, hospice workers, and caregivers—
Guide their healing actions and inspire their words and
spirit, most Loving Lord.

JOHN PREDMORE (1961–)
Jesuit priest and pastor in Amman, Jordan

A Prayer for the Human Family

O God, you made us in your own image and redeemed
us through Jesus your Son: Look with compassion on the
whole human family; take away the arrogance and hatred
which infect our hearts; break down the walls that separate

us; unite us in bonds of love; and work through our struggle
and confusion to accomplish your purposes on earth; that,
in your good time, all nations and races may serve you
in harmony around your heavenly throne; through Jesus
Christ our Lord.

Amen.

Adapted from *The Book of Common Prayer*

Save the Afflicted

We beseech thee, Master, to be our helper and protector.

Save the afflicted among us; have mercy on the lowly;
raise up the fallen; appear to the needy; heal the ungodly;
restore the wanderers of thy people; feed the hungry; ransom
our prisoners; raise up the sick; comfort the faint-hearted.

SAINT CLEMENT OF ROME (d. 99)
First bishop of Rome

A Prayer for All Nations

We pray, as we are taught, for all people, believing that this
is good and pleasing in the sight of God our Savior, who
desires all people to be saved and to come to the knowledge
of the truth and of Jesus Christ, who gave himself as a
ransom for all.

O look with compassion upon the world that lies in the
power of the evil one, and let the ruler of this world be cast
out, who has blinded their minds.

O let your way be known on earth, that barbarous
nations may be civilized, and those who live without God

in the world may be brought to the service of the living God; and thus, let your saving power be known among all nations. Let the peoples praise you, O God; yes, let all the peoples praise you: O let the nations be glad and sing for joy, for you judge the peoples with equity and guide the nations upon earth. O let your salvation and your righteousness be revealed in the sight of the nations, and let all the ends of the earth see the salvation of our God.

O make the nations your Son's heritage, and the ends of the earth his possession; let all the kingdoms of the world become the kingdom of the Lord and of his Christ.

MATTHEW HENRY (1662–1714)
Welsh minister and author

That Your Love Abound

And this is my prayer: that your love may abound more and more in knowledge and depth of insight, so that you may be able to discern what is best and may be pure and blameless for the day of Christ, filled with the fruit of righteousness that comes through Jesus Christ—to the glory and praise of God.

Philippians 1:9–11, NIV

Jesus Prays for His Disciples

My prayer is not for the world, but for those you have given me, because they belong to you. All who are mine belong to you, and you have given them to me, so they bring me glory. Now I am departing from the world; they are staying in this world, but I am coming to you. Holy Father, you have given me your name; now protect them by the power of your name so that they will be united just as we are. During my time here, I protected them by the power of the name you gave me. I guarded them so that not one was lost, except the one headed for destruction, as the Scriptures foretold.

Now I am coming to you. I told them many things while I was with them in this world so they would be filled with my joy. I have given them your word. And the world hates them because they do not belong to the world, just as I do not belong to the world. I'm not asking you to take them out of the world, but to keep them safe from the evil one. They do not belong to this world any more than I do. Make them holy by your truth; teach them your word, which is truth. Just as you sent me into the world, I am sending them into the world. And I give myself as a holy sacrifice for them so they can be made holy by your truth.

I am praying not only for these disciples but also for all who will ever believe in me through their message. I pray that they will all be one, just as you and I are one—as you are in me, Father, and I am in you. And may they be in us so that the world will believe you sent me.

I have given them the glory you gave me, so they may be one as we are one. I am in them and you are in me. May they experience such perfect unity that the world will know that you sent me and that you love them as much as you love me. Father, I want these whom you have given me to be with me where I am. Then they can see all the glory you gave me because you loved me even before the world began!

John 17:10–24, NLT

Moses Intercedes for the People

"Lord," he said, "why should your anger burn against your people, whom you brought out of Egypt with great power and a mighty hand? Why should the Egyptians say, 'It was with evil intent that he brought them out, to kill them in the mountains and to wipe them off the face of the earth'?

"Turn from your fierce anger; relent and do not bring disaster on your people. Remember your servants Abraham, Isaac and Israel, to whom you swore by your own self: 'I will make your descendants as numerous as the stars in the sky and I will give your descendants all this land I promised them, and it will be their inheritance forever.'"

Then the Lord relented and did not bring on his people the disaster he had threatened.

Exodus 32:11–14, NIV

For the Poor, the Oppressed, and the Prisoner

Almighty and most merciful God, we remember before you all poor and neglected persons whom it would be easy for us to forget: the homeless and the destitute, the old and the sick, and all who have none to care for them. Help us to heal those who are broken in body or spirit, and to turn their sorrow into joy. Grant this, Father, for the love of your Son, who for our sake became poor, Jesus Christ our Lord.

Look with pity, O heavenly Father, upon the people in this land who live with injustice, terror, disease, and death as their constant companions. Have mercy upon us. Help us to eliminate our cruelty to these our neighbors. Strengthen those who spend their lives establishing equal protection of the law and equal opportunities for all. And grant that every one of us may enjoy a fair portion of the riches of this land; through Jesus Christ our Lord.

Lord Jesus, for our sake you were condemned as a criminal: Visit our jails and prisons with your pity and judgment. Remember all prisoners, and bring the guilty to repentance and amendment of life according to your will, and give them hope for their future. When any are held unjustly, bring them release; forgive us, and teach us to improve our justice. Remember those who work in these institutions; keep them humane and compassionate; and save them from becoming brutal or callous. And since what we do for those in prison, O Lord, we do for you, constrain us to improve their lot. All this we ask for your mercy's sake. Amen.

Adapted from The Book of Common Prayer

Grant Mercy

Into your hands, merciful Lord, we commend ourselves for this day; may we be aware of your presence until its end; remind us that in whatever good we do we are serving you; make us careful and watchful, so that in everything we may discern your will, and, knowing it, may gladly obey.

Almighty and everlasting God, the comfort of the sad, the strength of those who suffer; hear the prayers of your children who cry out of any trouble; and to every distressed soul grant mercy, relief and refreshment.

Gelasian Sacramentary, eighth century

Rescue Those in Distress

We ask you, Master, be our helper and defender. Rescue those of our number in distress; raise up the fallen; assist the needy; heal the sick; turn back those of your people who stray; feed the hungry; release our captives; revive the weak; encourage those who lose heart.

Let all the nations realize that you are the only God, that Jesus Christ is your Child, and that we are your people and the sheep of your pasture.

SAINT CLEMENT OF ROME (d. 99)
First bishop of Rome

PRAYERS
⇢ *for* ⇠
SPECIAL DAYS
and OCCASIONS

This is the day the Lord has made;
We will rejoice and be glad in it.

<small>PSALM 118:24, NKJV</small>

Prayer
for a Wedding Day

....

The Seven Blessings

Blessed are You, Adonai, our God, Ruler of the Universe, Creator of the fruit of the vine.

Blessed are You, Adonai, our God, Ruler of the universe, Who has created everything for your glory.

Blessed are You, Adonai, our God, Ruler of the universe, Creator of Human Beings.

Blessed are You, Adonai, our God, Ruler of the universe, Who has fashioned human beings in your image, according to your likeness and has fashioned from it a lasting mold. Blessed are You Adonai, Creator of Human Beings.

Bring intense joy and exultation through the ingathering of Her children. Blessed are You, Adonai, are the One who gladdens Zion through Her children's return.

Gladden the beloved companions as You gladdened Your creatures in the garden of Eden. Blessed are You, Adonai, Who gladdens this couple.

Blessed are You, Adonai, our God, Ruler of the universe, Who created joy and gladness, loving couples, mirth, glad song, pleasure, delight, love, loving communities, peace, and companionship. Adonai, our God, let there soon be heard in the cities of Judah and the streets of Jerusalem the sound of joy and the sound of gladness, the voice of the loving couple, the sound of the their jubilance from their canopies and of the youths from their song-filled feasts.

Blessed are You Who causes the couple to rejoice, one with the other.

Traditional Jewish wedding blessing

Christmas Day

....

A Prayer for Christmas Morning

The day of joy returns, Father in Heaven, and crowns another year with peace and good will.

Help us rightly to remember the birth of Jesus, that we may share in the song of the angels, the gladness of the shepherds, and the worship of the wisemen.

Close the doors of hate and open the doors of love all over the world.

Let kindness come with every gift and good desires with every greeting.

Deliver us from evil, by the blessing that Christ brings, and teach us to be merry with clean hearts.

May the Christmas morning make us happy to be thy children, and the Christmas evening bring us to our bed with grateful thoughts, forgiving and forgiven, for Jesus' sake.

Amen.

HENRY VAN DYKE (1852–1933)
American author and minister

An Irish Christmas Blessing

God bless the corners of your house and all the lintels
    blessed.
And bless the hearth and bless the board and bless each
    place of rest,
And bless each door that opens wide to strangers as to kin,
And bless each crystal window pane that lets the starlight in,
And bless the rooftop overhead and every sturdy wall.
The peace of man. The peace of God. With peace and love
    for all.

Traditional Irish blessing

Adeste Fideles

O come, all ye faithful, joyful and triumphant!
O come ye, O come ye to Bethlehem;
Come and behold him
Born the King of Angels:
O come, let us adore Him,
O come, let us adore Him,
O come, let us adore Him,
Christ the Lord.

God of God, light of light,
Lo, he abhors not the Virgin's womb;
Very God, begotten, not created:
O come, let us adore Him,
O come, let us adore Him,
O come, let us adore Him,
Christ the Lord.

Sing, choirs of angels, sing in exultation,
Sing, all ye citizens of Heaven above!
Glory to God, glory in the highest:
O come, let us adore Him,
O come, let us adore Him,
O come, let us adore Him,
Christ the Lord.

Yea, Lord, we greet thee, born this happy morning;
Jesus, to thee be glory given!
Word of the Father, now in flesh appearing!
O come, let us adore Him,
O come, let us adore Him,
O come, let us adore Him,
Christ the Lord.

JOHN FRANCIS WADE (1711–1786)
English hymnist

Thanksgiving Day

Now Thank We All Our God

Now thank we all our God, with hearts and hands and voices;
Who wondrous things hath done, in whom this world
    rejoices.
Who, from our mother's arms, hath led us on our way,
With countless gifts of love, and still is ours today.

O may this bounteous God through all our life be near us,
With ever joyful hearts, and blessed peace to cheer us;
And keep still in grace, and guide us when perplexed;
And free us from all ills, in this world and the next.
All praise and thanks to God the Father now be given;
The Son and Him Who reigns with Them in highest heaven;
The one eternal God, Whom earth and heaven adore;
For thus it was, is now, and shall be evermore.

MARTIN RINKART (1586–1649)
Lutheran minister

Thanksgiving

For each new morning with its light,
For rest and shelter of the night,
For health and food,
For love and friends,
For everything Thy goodness sends.

RALPH WALDO EMERSON (1803–1882)
American poet

Easter

....

A Prayer for Easter Day

Christ is risen: The world below lies desolate.

Christ is risen: The spirits of evil are fallen.

Christ is risen: The angels of God are rejoicing.

Christ is risen: The tombs of the dead are empty.

Christ is risen indeed from the dead, the first of the sleepers.

Glory and power are his forever and ever,

Amen.

Saint Hippolytus (170–236)
Christian theologian

The Birth of a Child

....

Protect and Bless

O Sovereign Master and Lord Almighty, protect and bless this mother and this child. Shelter both under the covering of Your wings from this day forth.

Sovereign Master and Lord our God, Who was born of the Virgin Mary, Who as a Babe was laid in a manger, and as a Child was held up to be seen, do You Yourself preserve the child from every harm and the evils of this age.

O Lord our God, Who was well pleased to come down from the Heavens, and to be born of the Virgin Mary for the salvation of us sinners, be gracious to all the house in which the child has been born, granting forgiveness as our Good and Loving God; for You alone have the power to forgive sins, through the intercessions of the Holy Spirit and of all Your Saints. Forgive all voluntary and involuntary sin.

You are due all glory, honor, and adoration, to the Father, and to the Son, and to the Holy Spirit, both now and ever, and to the ages of ages.

Amen.

Adapted from the Greek Orthodox Liturgy

Bless This Son

May you be like Ephraim and Menashe.

Y'varekh'kha Adonai v'yishmerekha.
May Adonai bless you and keep you.

Ya'er Adonai panav eleikha vichunekka.
May Adonai make his face shine on you and show you his favor.

Yissa Adonai panav eleikha v'yasem l'kha shalom.
May Adonai lift up his face toward you and give you peace.

Traditional Jewish blessing
From Numbers 6:24–26, CJB

Bless This Daughter

May you be like Sarah, Rebecca, Rachel, and Leah.

Y'varekh'kha Adonai v'yishmerekha.
May Adonai bless you and keep you.

Ya'er Adonai panav eleikha vichunekka.
May Adonai make his face shine on you and show you his favor.

Yissa Adonai panav eleikha v'yasem l'kha shalom.
May Adonai lift up his face toward you and give you peace.

Traditional Jewish blessing
From Numbers 6:24–26, CJB

A Birthday Prayer

As I Begin Another Year

O God, my time on earth is in your hand. Look with favor, I pray, as I begin another year. Grant that I may continue to grow in wisdom and grace. Strengthen my trust in your goodness all the days of my life. Grant me comfort when I am discouraged or sorrowful; raise me up if I fall.

May your peace which surpasses all understanding abide with me all the days of my life, through Jesus Christ our Lord.

Amen.

Adapted from *The Book of Common Prayer*

YOUTH
~ *and* ~
CHILDREN'S
PRAYERS

But Jesus said, "Let the children come to me. Don't stop them! For the Kingdom of Heaven belongs to those who are like these children."

MATTHEW 19:14, NLT

Children's Bedtime Prayers

....

Now I Lay Me

Now I lay me down to sleep,
I pray the Lord my soul to keep.
If I should die before I wake,
I pray the Lord my soul to take.
Amen.

Eighteenth century

Angel of God

Angel of God, my Guardian dear,
To whom God's love commits me here;
Ever this day, be at my side
To light and guard, to rule and guide.

Traditional Catholic prayer

We Thank Thee for the Night

Father, we thank thee for the night,
And for the pleasant morning light;
For rest and food and loving care,
And all that makes the day so fair.
Help us to do the things we should,
To be to others kind and good;
In all we do, in work or play,
To grow more loving every day.

REBECCA J. WESTON
American hymnist

I Know that God Is Near

I hear no voice, I feel no touch,
I see no glory bright;
But yet I know that God is near,
In darkness as in light.

AUTHOR UNKNOWN

Children's Prayers at Mealtime

God Is Great

God is great and God is Good,
And we thank God for our food;
By God's hand we must be fed,
Give us Lord, our daily bread.
Amen.

P.P. BLISS (1838–1876)
American songwriter and composer

Thank You, God

Thank you for the world so sweet,
Thank you for the food we eat.
Thank you for the birds that sing,
Thank you, God, for everything.
Amen.

AUTHOR UNKNOWN

Children's Morning Prayers

Before I Run to Play

Now, before I run to play,
Let me not forget to pray
To God who kept me through the night
And waked me with the morning light.
Help me, Lord, to love thee more
Than I ever loved before,
In my work and in my play
Be thou with me through the day.
Amen.

AUTHOR UNKNOWN

I Start Each Day

Lord, in the morning I start each day,
By taking a moment to bow and pray.
I start with thanks, and then give praise
For all your kind and loving ways.
Today if sunshine turns to rain,
If a dark cloud brings some pain,
I won't doubt or hide in fear
For you, my God, are always near.
I will travel where you lead;
I will help my friends in need.
Where you send me I will go;
With your help I'll learn and grow.
Hold my family in your hands,

As we follow your commands.
And I will keep you close in sight
Until I crawl in bed tonight.
Amen.

MARY FAIRCHILD (1855–1921)
Pioneering American librarian

A Favorite Song for Children

....

Jesus Loves Me

Jesus loves me! This I know,
For the Bible tells me so.
Little ones to Him belong;
They are weak, but He is strong.

Jesus loves me! This I know,
As He loved so long ago,
Taking children on His knee,
Saying, "Let them come to Me."

Jesus loves me still today,
Walking with me on my way,
Wanting as a friend to give
Light and love to all who live.

Jesus loves me! He who died
Heaven's gate to open wide;
He will wash away my sin,
Let His little child come in.

Jesus loves me! He will stay
Close beside me all the way;
Thou hast bled and died for me,
I will henceforth live for Thee.

Yes, Jesus loves me!
Yes, Jesus loves me!
Yes, Jesus loves me!
The Bible tells me so.

ANNA BARTLETT WARNER (1827–1915)
American author and poet

A Student's Prayer

God of Light and Truth, thank you for giving me a mind
that can know and a heart that can love.

Help me to keep learning every day of my life, for all
knowledge leads to you.

Let me be aware of your presence in all things and at
all times.

Encourage me when work is difficult and when I am
tempted to give up; encourage me when my brain seems
slow and the way forward is difficult.

Grant me the grace to put my mind to use exploring
the world you have created, confident that in you there a
wisdom that is real.

Amen.

AUTHOR UNKNOWN

THEME INDEX

AUTHOR INDEX

SCRIPTURE INDEX

ABOUT THE AUTHOR

Mark Gilroy has more than thirty years of experience
in the publishing industry. He served as senior
vice president of Integrity Publishing and has held
positions at Albury Publishing Company, RiverOak
Publishing, and Nazarene Publishing House. His
books include *Spending Time with God*, a devotional
guide for teens; *Loving the Love of Your Life*, an
inspirational guide for couples; and *How Great is Our
God: Classic Writings from History's Greatest Christian
Thinkers in Contemporary Language*. He holds B.A.s
in Biblical Literature and Speech Communications,
an M.B.A. from Baker University, and an M.Div. from
Nazarene Theological Seminary. He has also written
the novels *Cold As Ice, Cuts Like a Knife, Every Breath
You Take,* and *Just Before Midnight.* Learn more about
Mark at www.markgilroy.com.